Margie' Hubbard's

The Gift

Poetry for Everyday Meditation

by

Margie Hubbard

Copyright © Margie Hubbard

All rights reserved. No part of this publication may be reproduced, distributed, or transmitted in any form or by any means, including photocopying, recording, or other electronic or mechanical methods, without the prior written permission of the publisher, except in the case of brief quotations embodied in critical reviews and certain other noncommercial uses permitted by copyright law.

ISBN-978-1-951300-14-2

Liberation's Publishing LLC
West Point - Mississippi

Margie' Hubbard's
The
Gift

Poetry for Everyday Meditation

Contents

He's Got the Whole World 6

Peer & Pressure the Twins 8

Who Am I? 10

Don't Stop Your Mission 12

The Right Direction 14

Faith 15

A Thanks From The Heart 16

Winning Day 18

No Knife, No Gun 20

Worry 21

God, You've Been Good to Me 22

I Know A Place 23

Claiming Your Blessings 24

Remember Jesus Everyday 25

The Feeling of Feeling Like 26

New Bethel's Prayer #1 28

Welcome 30

A Prayer to Cleanse 31

Lord 32

A Prayer of Confession 34

My Hug 36

Stuck In The Mud	37
Praise In Advance	38
Saturday August 3, 2013	40
Margie's Hope List	41
A Message From Heaven	42
Guess Who Poem	44
A Prayer for Mom & Dad	46
A Save From God Threw Joshua	48
April 22, 2015	50
April 7th 2015	52
I Need An Answer Lord	54
There Is A Need	55
A Letter To God	56
Another Job	57
A Prayer For LaVontis	58
Let Go, Let God	60
Power Restored	62
Perfect Peace	64
To You Lord	66
True Worship	68
If We All Could Get Together,	69
What a Time	69
A Mother's Job	70
A Word of Thanks	71

Easter Speech 72

Memorial Day 73

Sunday Before Christmas 2007 74

Merry Christmas From Joe & Margie 76

Christmas 2010 77

The Sunday Before Christmas 2018 78

This book is dedicated to
My Lord and Savior Jesus Christ!

He's Got the Whole World

Hello everyone
God has taken a stand.
To let us all, know that
He's got the whole world in his hands.
He's got the boy the girl
The woman and the man.
He's got the whole world
In His hands.
He's got the cure for COVID, Aids
Sickness all over the lands
He's got the whole world
In His hands.
He' got the leader, the background
And the whole entire band.
He's got the whole world in His Hands.
He's got the people across the waters
And the people across the sands.
He's got the whole world
In His hands.
He's got the people on the beach
Even the ones getting a tan.
He's got the whole world in his hands.
He's got the animals, the trees
the water, grass and the land.
He's got the whole world
In His hands
He's got the furniture, homes the vehicles
The commodes, rugs, and ceiling fans

He's got the whole world
in His hands
He got us when we're happy or sad
When we know or when we don't understand.
He's got the whole world
in His hands
We can look at ourselves as small,
medium, big, or grand,
But He's got the whole world
in His Hands
We might be a housewife, schoolteacher,
Homeless, Dr. Lawyer or even a rich businessman.
But just know He's got the whole world
In his hands.
You can drive a bus, a car, a plane, a boat, train
truck or even a van.
But He's got the whole world
In His hand.
You can use a conjunction word
But, because, although, or, and.
But just know he's got the whole world
In His hands.
So, we must do right
And pray when we can.
And just know that God's got the whole world
In His hands.

Margie Hubbard

Peer & Pressure the Twins

Hello there world
Let me talk to you.
I forgot to tell you.
What peer pressure will do
It will make you feel
That it really exists.
It will study your life
And get all up in the mist
Peer will act as your best friend
It will do that at first.
Then pressure will push you to the limit
Until your body gets a thirst.
I've been there to
I know how it can be.
They will have you jumping here and there
Like a bad little flee.
It can come in form of a sister
Brother and cousin too.
It can even be your best friend.
Lol it can even be your boo.
Now to get that cure that you need
Is to keep this in mind.
It's like your mom and dad said
You're going to need Jesus at all times.

Matthew 6:33 says; "Seek ye first
No matter where you go.
On the road, in your home,
When you're happy or feeling Low.
So, pray in season
And out of season too.
Pray for your friends and your family
And don't forget your boo.
When you seek ye first the kingdom of God
All other things will be added unto you.
You can't beat that with nobody's stick
No matter what you do.

Who Am I?

Hey boys and girls
Across the land.
Try to guess who I am
That if you can.
The first clue I'll give you
Is the whitest of white.
Make sure all the stains
Has been taken out of sight.
The reason for my name is
Because there's a place I've never been.
By being the person that I am
I've been made fun of by some friends.
But I'm happy right now
Not for fame or wealth.
It's a good place to be.
If you're thinking about your health.
God wants you to be like I am
And this is a fact.
Because if you go any further
You cannot go back.
You can try it if you want
You can try it if you may.
But you could never be the same
As you were before that day.

I don't worry about drugs or sex
I don't worry about fame.
These are two things
That could change my name.
So, study God's word
Try to keep his commands.
And try to be like me
For as long as you can.
Now this is the end of my rhyme
I hope you've guessed who.
Remember God loves all
And I do too.

Don't Stop Your Mission

Life is a mission
Here on this earth.
And the mission began
The day of your birth
So don't stop your mission.
Though your mission can get hard
In the days ahead
So bad that sometimes
you might wish you were dead.
But don't stop this mission.
You might feel like your friends
Have just let you down
Some might think
They have no friend in town
You still can't stop your mission
You might feel like you're climbing
Out of the bottomless pit.
And you're feeling tired
And Satan says, just quit.
Please don't stop your mission.
When you can't charge new shoes
Or a new little black dress.
Because your credit card
Is already a mess.

Don't stop the mission.
When you went in the store
And bought the perfect three-piece suit.
But you didn't have enough money
To buy the matching pair of shoes or boots.
Don't give up on the mission.
When your medicine bottle is empty
And you have no pills
And you can't afford the copay
To get the bottles refilled
Don't stop the mission
Although life circumstances
Have a lot of demands.
Some of which
We don't understand.
But don't stop your mission
So, if we want to add
To our church organism
We must go out
And do some evangelism
Oh yes, hold on to your mission

Margie Hubbard

The Right Direction

Good evening to all
Mothers, fathers, sisters, brothers, and friends
We've almost came
To another year's end.
We welcome you to take a step
Over in the right direction.
You don't have to vote on it
Or hold an election.
But it's off with the bad
And on with the good.
It's on living our lives
Like we know we should.
Its families worshiping together
In spirit and in truth.
Like it was explained to us
In the bible book of Ruth.
So, let's do right and live right
Is my advice.
Then we can live in heaven for eternity.
With our Lord and Savior Jesus Christ.

Faith

This substance of things to hope for
This evidence of things not seen.
This is what Hebrews 11;1 tells us
That faith really means.
Now webster on the other hand
Had this to say.
Faith is belief without proof
This meaning is still okay.
God wants us to have faith
If just only the size of a mustard seed.
And he will work miracles
And do us good deeds.
Faith can move mountains
That you wouldn't believe.
Through faith god
Will help us succeed.
Oh yes with faith
God has done so much for me.
He always has a light
To make sure I can see.
So always have faith
In your heart and life.
Then you can know everything is alright
And you don't have to think twice.

A Thanks From The Heart

Thanks, you World Changers
For all that you do
You helped the Hubbard family
By letting God bless us through you.
The group that was here
Was awesome as could be.
They painted and trimmed everything
Down to the tee.
They were more like family
Not just our friends
They treated us with respect
From start to end.
Mr. John and Mrs. Tammy were a blessing
From the very start.
And the young men and women stole
Mr. Hubbard and my heart.
So, hats off to The Hard Hats
For everything they did.
I want to be just like them
When I get big.
Keep doing what you're doing world changers
Always pray when you can.
And never let go
Of god's unchanging hand.

This is the end of our rhyme
Right here I'll quit
Because when it comes to The World Changers
This isn't the half of it

Winning Day

I was sitting around on Saturday
July the 9th two thousand and five.
When is seem like all my thoughts?
Had begun to come alive.
I thought of things
That was going on in my life.
I felt like my heart
Had been cut in half with a knife.
So now I'm wondering
What is it I am going to do?
My heart hurting, feeling bad
Feel like crying too.
Then came the devil
Putting thought here and there.
Trying to make me feel
That nobody even cares.
I admit that at one point
Satan was doing his job well
But then God put a thought in my mind
That more than likely saved me from hell.
Because I'm thinking of this and that
All over the place.
Like when you thought you hit a home run
But only made it to second base.

But now here comes Jesus
And he's coming up to bat.
He's already taken away
That old this and that.
He's taken away old worry
And the knife from the heart.
Halleluiah Jesus hit the ball
All the way out of the park
Here's what will happen
If you let Jesus have his way.
He can change the losing moment
Into a winning day.

No Knife, No Gun

Our Father, who are in heaven
Yes, it's me again.
Asking you Lord, if it be thy will.
To forgive me of my sins.
For theirs something that's bugging me
And I don't know what it's about.
I feel like sometimes like opening my mouth
And letting out a shout.
Seems like the weight of the world
Is on my back and crashing me down.
And it's getting kind of hard
To wear a smile on top of a frown.
But Lord I know with you on my side
I know my battle can be won.
I don't need no bow-n-arrow, or knife
Nor do I need a gun.
My joy, peace, Father and friend.
You'll stick closer than a brother
You'll be there until the end

Worry

I'm going to talk to you
Without any hurry.
Of a condition we have
it's called worry.
We should not do it
But we sometimes do.
I'm guilty of doing it
And so are you.
We worry about tomorrow
And it's not promised to us.
Of doing this and that
And making a lot of fuss.
So, we should read
St. John 14;1-3.
It should stop the worry
For you and me.
So, let not your heart be troubled
As God has said.
Then we can rest better
When we get into our beds.

God, You've Been Good to Me

I was just sitting down chilling
on Saturday November 21, 2009.
When a lot of things
began to tumble through my mind.
I thought of how good God has been to me
Down through the years.
He has made a lot of laughter
out of a lot of tears.
He has picked me up
and turned me around.
He has made smiles out of so many frowns.
There is only one thing
That our God can do.
He will never fail
for me and for you
So now I'm saying, Lord
make my heart right.
I ask this in Jesus' name
this very night.
Help me to be
as you want me too
Show me and help me
To do as you'd want me to do.
Amen

I Know A Place

I know a place to go
Where love never ends.
And I know a place to go
Where souls have no sin.
I know a place to go
There's happiness every day.
And I know a place to go
But to go there we must pray
I know a place to go
Where souls are all at peace
I know a place
Where prayers never cease.
Heaven, heaven, heaven
Is where I'm going to be.
So, you won't hear a sound
from the corps in the ground
I'm In heaven for eternity.

Claiming Your Blessings

Greeting to all
For this is true.
God has a blessing
Just waiting for you.
So, you don't have to worry
You don't have to fret.
God isn't through
Blessing you yet.
Psalm 37:4 says "delight yourself
Also, in the lord
And he shall give you
The desires of your heart
So, ask for it in faith
Claim your victory.
Then god will bless you
And your family abundantly.

Remember Jesus Everyday

Joy to the world
The lord has come.
Today is the day we celebrate
The day Jesus was born.
It's not the presents or Santa
No not even the Christmas tree.
It's our Savior that was born
To save both you and me.
So, have a merry Christmas
And remember what I say.
Don't only remember Jesus on December 25
Remember Him every day.

The Feeling of Feeling Like

I have a feeling
It's like really deep.
When I let my guard down
It sometimes gives me the creeps.
It feels like sometimes
I'm not doing enough.
It seems like when I try to do things
Life gets really tough
It seems like my shoulders
Are carrying the weight of the world.
Like when you're driving down the road
And you slide in a curve.
I know that this feeling
Is not one that's right?
Because when you know God.
It will make a dark day turn bright.
James 1:2 says to count it all joy
When we face trials of any kind.
God can change these feelings
Like he changed water into wine.
These feelings I'm having
Are just a part of life's up and downs.
But I can't go here and there
With a sad old ugly frown.

I have to call on Jesus
Just like He said
Then I will be able
To clear my head.

New Bethel's Prayer #1

Our father in heaven
To you I pray.
That you will continue to bless New Bethel
Each and every day,
Bless the walls
So firm and stout.
And please keep confusion
And bitterness out.
Bless Pastor Fisher and his family
And the congregation too.
We're already blessed Lord
With how you do the things You do.
We pray that you Lord
Bring back all the members.
We ask this in Jesus' name
Before the end of December.
Bless all of the choirs
As they sing praises to Your name.
Let's all praise You
But not for shape, form, or fame.
Bless all the ministries
And the bus ministry too.
Bless the mower and cleaning ministry
For even doing what they do.

Keep the mics and amps system
So, the words can be heard loud and clear
We need to hear the word
Because Your coming back
Is growing near.
New bethel is happy with you Jesus
We're happy with you alone.
We want You to know this
As we sing our songs.
So, let the Spirit fall fresh
On every boy, girl, woman, and man.
We got to wait on you Lord
Because you have the master plan.
So, open the flood gates of heaven
That's what Bishop Paul Martin say.
Let it rain down your blessings Lord
Day after day after day.

Welcome

Hello everyone
I came to say
You are welcome to our
Youth choir Anniversary today.
Welcome once welcome twice
Welcome three and four
If that's not welcome enough
You are welcome once more.
Welcome, welcome, welcome

A Prayer to Cleanse

Dear Lord
To you I pray.
Help me to understand
All your directions each and every way.
I need the wisdom
In my heart and soul.
So, I can speak
Tall, proud and bold.
I need you Lord
Please guide my heart.
And from me Dear Lord
Never ever depart
Our father in heaven
Get in my body, soul, and mind.
Help me think and do positive things
Leaving the garbage behind.
Now I'm a new person
Because God has created in me.
A clean heart
Like it should always be.

Margie Hubbard

Lord

Lord I can't help
But to say.
You bless me to see
One more day.
I couldn't have done it
By myself.
Without your sacrifice
None of us would be left.
Without you Lord I'm like a ship
Without a sail
Without You Lord I would spend
Eternal life in hell.
So, create in me
A clean, clean heart.
Get in my mind and body
And from me never ever depart.
For you picked me up
And you turned me around.
Lord; you know you put my feet
Upon solid ground.
Now I see a little clearer
Then I did yesterday.
Because you Lord
Made everything okay.

Now I end my rhyme
Right here I'll quit.
Because when I talk about the Lord
This isn't the half of it.

A Prayer of Confession

Our father in heaven
It's Margie again.
This prayer is for this world
Asking for forgiveness for all our sins.
Lord we sin in the morning
Lord we even sin at night.
Lord a lot of us sin believing
That you'll say it's alright.
Lord we think bad things
With this we think we'll get by.
But on that Day of judgment
It'll be too late to cry.
Some of us think that we can
Buy our way into heaven.
But thinking this is only a gamble
With no lucky number seven
Some of us think
That we can wish upon a star
You can try It if you want
You'll wake up not pleased with where you are
We sometimes ask the fortuneteller
Where are we going to go?
You can ask God for free
He's the only one who knows.

So, as we deal
With life's temptations.
Remember Jesus'
Death and resurrection
He didn't hang
On the cross for fun.
He did it for the sins
Of everyone.
So, thank you lord for everything
That you're doing and have done.
And here's a special thanks
For all our battles you won

My Hug

Hello lord
Yes, it's me again.
Right now, I really need
A hug from my best friend.
I can't really say
What's wrong with me.
But I know I'm feeling
As down as can be.
So, lord please forgive me
For feeling like I do.
Because You've blessed me
And I give all praises to you.
Now I'm feeling the hug
The hug I truly needed.
For my heart is feeling the joy right now
The joy that I know I can succeed.
Now thank you lord for my blessing
Once again lord, you came through.
You gave me what I asked for and I needed
So, Hallelujah Lord, all praises to you.

Stuck In The Mud

Dear lord
We need to talk.
I feel like we're at a stand still
Stuck in the mud like a corn stalk
Had to buy groceries
Bank account almost over drawn.
And I sure don't need bill collectors
Calling me on my phone.
Even with all of this going on
You're blessing us though
You even watched over us
As we traveled to and fro.
You were there with us
Even before we were born.
Dear lord I know
You'll never leave us alone.
So why should I worry
Why should I fret?
There's no need for me
To get all upset.
So, lord I'm putting everything
Lord, in your hands.
Because if anyone can fix it
Lord I know you can.

Praise In Advance

Dear lord
I had the need to say.
Thank you, Dear Lord,
For one more day.
You've blessed me through
Dangers of seen and unseen.
And from people that
Just want to be mean
Lord, you know
I can't thank you enough.
You were there
When times got tough.
You bless me with
So much Lord.
My husband, children, and grandchildren
Are all special gifts from you God.
I pray to
Do your will.
I want to walk the way you want me to walk
And live the way you want me to live.
So, I'm praising you
In advance.
That you will show me
In a glance.

Now I thank you Lord
Once again.
My savior, Lawyer, Doctor, Father
Provider, Deliverer, and Friend.
I close my rhyme
But my prayer will NOT end.
And until next time lord
I love you Amen.

Saturday August 3, 2013

I was sitting in my home
Saturday August 3, 2013.
My mine roaming here and there
Like a book that had no theme.
I didn't know what road I would take
Didn't know which way to go.
But God had all the directions I needed
To take me to and fro.
I just had to give it to Jesus
That's all I had to do.
He's someone that will help a sister or a brother
And I know he'll help me to.
So now Lord, here's my mind
Heart, and my soul too.
Now put me in the direction Lord
That's real pleasing to You.
Thank You Lord

Margie's Hope List

Hello my children
Let's cut the chase.
My life with you-all
I would never erase.
I know I don't always say it
But I love you-all, I do.
And I'm glad that God
Blessed me with the five of you.
You know life goes by fast
As quick as a slap on the risk.
That's why I'm giving you-all
A copy of Margie's hope list.
I hope my children will always
Keep peace and love for each other.
The love and peace that God wants
Between every sister and brother.
I hope you will respect other people
Not some of the time but always.
Doing this alone
Will lengthen you days

A Message From Heaven

Hello my cousins
For this I say it's true.
When I was down there
I enjoyed the times with you.
You know the songs I sang
I was letting you-all know.
That I was preparing myself
Because I was getting ready to go.
You probably remember the times we played
And my laughs and smile
But one thing we have in common
We're only here for a little while
My mind was made up
You got to make yours up too.
You got to determine what's important
Live with your mind on "What will Jesus do?"
Let go of your life
Just let go and let God.
He knows when
And how to fix your heart.
You don't have to wonder or think
Or anticipate.
Just work for Jesus
Don't let it be too late.

You're probably wondering
Why did I get this, why me?
But you got time to get it right
And be the best that you can be.
God said, "If my people who are called by my name
Would pray" then He would heal the land.
So, you got to get in a hurry
You got to do what you can.
Well it's about time
Time for me to go
I now sing on
The heavenly choir you know.
But here's one last thing
That I would like to say.
No matter what you decided to do
Before you do it, always remember to pray.
Then you can feel like the birds
And you can do like me.
You can take two wings and fly away to glory
And live free for eternity.
Love y'all Punkin

Guess Who Poem

Cars began to pile up
Everywhere in sight.
But this black man
Invented the traffic light. Garret Morgan
Then things looked blurry for all us blacks
Or so it may seem.
Until this black man said
Yes, I have a dream. Martin L king
I am the first black mayor
In the little Maben town.
In a place where most of us
Used to hang around. Larry Pruitt
Ole Miss is the college where I went
And there I was really smart
It was there I was the first black women
To get this award. Tessa Burchfield
I don't have to worry about money
I have plenty laying around.
Because I'm the richest black women
There is in town. Oprah Winfrey
This is the end of my guess who poem
Your time was well spent.
Before I go, I'd like to introduce
Our first black president.

Barak Obama in his name
Of this distinguished man.
He won the election with faith
Saying, yes we can.
But as we all know
This wouldn't come true.
If it hadn't been for the Lord
He blessed these people, me and He blessed you.

A Prayer for Mom & Dad

Our Father in heaven
To you Lord I pray.
That you will bless the mothers and fathers.
Each and Every day.
Give them the power Lord
To do your will.
And the strength they need
to climb the rugged hill.
Help their hands Lord
To prepare the best meals.
And when they travel down the roads
Lord guide their steering wheels.
Lord put your arms around them
Protect their whole family.
And bless them oh Lord
Bless them abundantly.
Forgive them Lord
For all their sins.
Renew them Lord
With a heart that's been cleansed.
Bless their home
With blessings from above.
And make sure you rain down
Showers of peace, joy, and love.

We pray for a happy home
Bless their going out and coming in.
This prayer we pray in Jesus name
Now let us all say A-men.

A Save From God Threw Joshua

Sitting here this Friday night
Two thousand and ten.
Thinking about the more I try
The harder it is to win.
It feels like I'm walking up a mountain
With no end in sight.
I'm trying hard as can be
With all my might.
I feel helpless in a way
Like I can't do anything.
Like when someone gives you instructions
And you don't know what they mean.
Then I begin to be afraid
Of the thing to come.
But then Joshua 1:9 came to mind
And exploded like a bomb.
Joshua said, "Be not afraid or dismayed
For the Lord is with us.
So, we don't have to worry
Or even make a fuss.
We don't have to worry
We don't have to fret.
God is still with us.
He hasn't left us yet.

So now my directions
Are all written to the tee?
So, when I'm feeling like this again
I know that God is with me.

April 22, 2015

It's Wednesday night
April 22, 2015
Lord help me to say
What I really mean.
Lord I haven't been
What I should.
Nor have I done
What I could.
I haven't said
What I need.
And lately I haven't tried
To succeed.
I haven't visited
any of the sick
And I know
I must do this quick.
Time is winding down
I know this is true.
So please help me Lord
To do what you need me to do.
I ask this Lord
If it's in your will.
That you will help me love like you want me to
And to give like you want me to give.

There's one last thing in this poem
That I'm going to ask you
Please forgive me
For not, doing what I was supposed to do.

April 7th 2015

As I lay in bed
April 7, 2015.
Feeling kind of down
Or so it may seem.
Lord I need
Your warm embrace.
And this time Lord
Will you please make haste?
I've tried to do
Everything that's all right.
But I know I haven't given it
All my might.
That's probably why everything
Looks like it's going uphill.
Like when you took an aspirin
But needed a blood pressure pill.
You always know Lord
Just what I need.
All I must do
Is to have faith and believe.
So have mercy on me Lord
As David said
Make me whole again
Before I go to sleep in my bed

Right here I lay everything
Lord at your feet.
I know at the end
Everything will be nice and neat.
Just like now lord
You've already worked it out.
Now I ask myself
Margie Ruth, what are you worried about?
Thank you, Lord.

I Need An Answer Lord

I need an answer Lord
To what I'm going to do.
I can't make a decision
Without first talking to you.
I don't like making trouble
With anyone anywhere.
So, show me what I can do
To make things better there.
Is my time over doing this?
Please let me know,
But if it means keeping peace
I will let it go.
So, I'm giving it to you Lord
To do what is in your will
Now I won't have to worry about it
Or make myself get ill.
Lord I thank you
For all your love and care.
When I pray about a situation
My answer is always there.
Hallelujah, Hallelujah, Hallelujah
To the god above all,
Thank you, and I love you
And you always hear your calls.

There Is A Need

Listen my people
All over this world.
There are starving
Men, women, boys and girls.
We can't sit around
With our heads up high.
Like we haven't been blessed
Down from the sky.
So, come on my people
Let's get together and see.
How we can make a difference
For each family
I said this once
And I'll say it again.
God wants us all
to be good friends.
So, bless all of us Lord
As we go on our way.
Build us up where we are weak
And make us stronger every day.

A Letter To God

Dear lord
Let's have a talk
First, I want to thank you
For being with me through this walk
Things have really changed
And put our mind to wonder.
What's going to happen next?
Our minds are at a ponder.
Is this going to carry us out?
Is it close to the end?
I do know without a shower of a doubt
It's closer than it's ever been.
With all the questions we have
Some of the answers we don't know.
But Lord you're in control of everything
That we know for show
With that said Lord
I don't have to worry; I don't have to fret.
You promise you will always be with us.
You haven't left us yet.
I thank you Lord
And without further ado.
I love you Lord and
Hallelujah, Hallelujah, Hallelujah to you.

Another Job

Dear Lord
To you I pray.
I know that you're going to bless me
With another job someday.
But I must be patient
and give it a little time.
Because I've already did my prayer
Now I'm waiting on the job of mine.
For Lord, I thank you for this job
Don't think I don't.
But I feel it's time to leave now
But if it's not time Lord, I won't.

A Prayer For LaVontis

Dear Lord
To You we pray.
That you will watch over LaVonits
Each and every day.
Watch over his whole body
Keep his arteries and bones just right.
Watch over him while he's practicing
Every day and every night.
Bless the tires Lord
As he travels to and fro.
We may not think of everything
But Lord we know you know
Bless his food Lord
in case he forgets to pray
put a shield of protection over everything Lord
We got to keep Von okay.
Protect the bed and dorm room
In which he must sleep.
Give him a happy heart
So, he won't have time to weep.
We pray this prayer for everyone there
We pray a blessing for all of them through and
through.
But none of this can happen Lord

Unless it comes from You.
Now thank you Lord for Everything
And for you Lord, we'll always stand.
This prayer we pray in your name Lord
And we all say A-men.

Let Go, Let God

Hi everyone
I need to talk to you for a while
Sometimes in our life
Might seem to cramp our style
A lot of things
Might be going on in our life
Wondering if you're doing things right
Sometimes you have to think twice
It seems like
You're running out of time
All kinds of negative stuff
Bouncing around in your mind
Now you're at the crossroads
And you now have a choice to make
Being with family and friends
And the smile you have to fake
Lord where do I go from here
That's the next big question
You feel stuck in the mud
Waiting for a sense of direction
You think you have it down pack
But then there comes the brick wall
But God is always standing there
waiting on your call

Matthew 7:7 says, "Ask and it shall be given"
Verse 8 says "Seek ye shall find"
But you're sitting with your head down
With a million things going through your mind
And then here comes
the four words you need
Let go, Let God
And then you will succeed

Power Restored

I was lying in bed
Saturday October 12, 2013
Pondering over what's going on
And trying to figure what it means
I then got up
To read and meditate
So God would open up
My spiritual gate
I started with prayer
To invite God in
To set, guide, and teach me
Because he's my guide and my friend
He carried me to Isaiah 40
I didn't know why
That's when strength, power, and comfort
Appeared to my eyes
I needed all of that
That very day
And all I had to do was have faith
When I sat down to pray
Isaiah 40:29 said, "The Lord gives power to the faint."
He'll increase strength if you have no might
These are things we all need

On this spiritual fight
So keep God with you
No matter where you're at
He was Israel's Incomparable God
And Today He's still all of that
Job 38:41 ask, "Who provided the raven his food
when his young cry unto the Lord?"
It was none
But God
Isaiah 40:12, "Who measured the waters
I the hollow of his hands.
And meted out heaven with the span.
God will give you strength
comfort and power
And He can do all of this
No matter what hour
So always keep this
in your mind
God is always and will always be
Right on time

Perfect Peace

Hello world
For this I say is true
Sometimes the trials of life
May seem dim to me and you
We may try a higher watt bulb
To make the day seem bright
Be we still find ourselves
Searching even harder for light
We open up the blinds
All over our home
But it seems like light
Has packed up and gone
Where are you brighter day?
I'm searching far and wide
But you don't see it anywhere
Not even outside
But this is how Satan wants us to feel
But this isn't how God say do it
He wants us to keep believing
and never ever quit
Joshua 1:9 said, "Be not afraid or dismayed
for I am with you"
And at the same time
He's with everyone else too

It's enough of Him
To go all around
He's bigger than all the waters
He's bigger than all the grounds
Isn't it good to know Jesus
Your God and mine
When our trials get hard to bare
Call him He's right on time
I know you know about prayer
I know about prayer too
And God is going to work it out
For me and for you
Because here's what will happen
When our prayers don't cease
God can put our health, mind, and life
Back in Perfect Peace!

To You Lord

I've looked in the back of my mind
To see what I can see
One thing I found
Is that God has been good to me
For all the lay off
He's carried me through
And all the other blessings
He has done for me too
I want to thank you Lord
With all of my heart
Through dangers, toils, and snares
You were with me from the start
There are some days
When I'm feeling kind of down
You put a smile
In place of my frown
I need you Lord
All though I've sinned
Create in me a clean heart
Make me whole again
Time is running out
I know this for sure
Jobs closing, children fighting parents
Diseases have no cures

So forgive me Lord
for all of my sins
Help me to love my enemies
As well as my friends
Bless everyone else
All over these lands
Keep your loving arms around us
Hold us with your unchanging hand

True Worship

I went online
To the dictionary search
I realized that true worship today
Is not the same as the early church
They worshipped with their hearts
They worshipped with their feet
Their worship didn't come from the surface
It came from down deep
Everything that has breath
Praise! Praise the Lord
Because all Christians back then
Were all on one accord
Everything they did was in order and neat
From singing, praying, and hand clapping
To the patting of their feet
They worshipped in Sunday School
The worshipped all the way through BTU
We should praise and worship God
In everything we do
So praise the Lord, praise ye the Lord
And also believe
And the Lord will rain down blessings
That we won't have room to receive

If We All Could Get Together, What a Time

Hello world
I'm dropping you a small line
Telling you if we could all get together
What a time, what a time, what a time
Some of us might move out of town
Or go off to school for a period of time
But if we could get back together
Oh! What a time, what a time, what a time
This is to everyone all over this world
I hope ya'll are well and doing fine
The thought of us being together again
Ooo! What a time, What a time, What a time
We are all God's creation
Born from King David's bloodline
And if we could all get together
Yes! What a time, what a time, what a time
We need more love, peace, joe, and understanding
In all your hearts and mind
With prayer God will get us together
And you guessed it
What a time, what a time, what a time

A Mother's Job

A mother's job
Is hard you see
She has to help dad
To take care of me
She washes our clothes
And combs our hair
She mends our clothes
Whenever they tare
She wakes us up early
Gets us ready for school
She always tells us to be good
And to obey the golden rule
So love your mother
And always treat her nice
Because if you think her job isn't hard
You'd better think twice

A Word of Thanks

Dear God
To you I pray
That my life with you is okay
I know Dear Lord
I'm not what I should
Please bless me to do your will
Like I know I could
So forgive me Lord
If it be thy Holy will
Create in me a clean heart
And show me how to live
Bless my husband Lord
And my children too
Teach us the right way to live
Please Lord guide us through
Look over everyone Lord
To you I pray
Thank you Lord for everything you've done
As we travel along the way
I love you Lord,
Amen

Easter Speech

I didn't come to give you a long speech
I just came to say.
Yes, you guessed it right
Happy Easter Day.
It's not the bunny
The egg or the hen.
That died on the cross
For our sins.
It's not all the candy
That fills the baskets.
It' our Lord and Savior Jesus Christ
That makes Easter fantastic.
Happy Easter

Memorial Day

Let's look back and reflect
On this church once again.
On some of the things we did
Way back when.
This church started
With a little brown shack,
It was small, but with spirit
And we thank God for that.
Although we didn't have a piano
Nor organ or drums.
But now we act like we can't sing
Unless we have some.
We'd pat our hands and stomp our feet
And we'd give praises to the lord.
We provided for one another
we prayed for each other
Because we were all on one accord.
I'll stop right here
But there is plenty more to say.
So, let's get in service and praise the Lord
Like we did in the old-time way

Sunday Before Christmas 2007

Twas the Sunday before Christmas
When all through New Bethels church house.
Everybody was singing and rejoicing
No one was quiet as a mouse.
As the devotion got started
Who would appear?
No it wasn't Santa
Nor the eight tiny reindeer.
The Lord had showed up
And we knew He would show out.
As He began throwing miracles
Around and about.
The mothers all sang
And the deacons did the prayers.
They did it from their hearts
Because they knew the Lord was there.
Pastor Fisher was in the pulpit
With a word from the Lord.
Blessing are what the New Bethel got that day.
Because we were all on one accord.
The Holy Spirit would move that day
From one person to the other.
He would move on all the fathers
He would move on all the mothers.

The choir was in harmony
And the ushers wore a smile.
The Lord is surely in this place
Stacking blessings in a pile.
Yes, this all happened
The Sunday before Christmas 2007.
And if we keep doing this New Bethel
We can all have church together in heaven.
Yes, everybody was happy
And of good sheer.
Merry Christmas from New Bethel
And a Happy New Year.

Merry Christmas From Joe & Margie

Hello everyone
Let's all unwind
Tis the season to be jolly
It's almost Christmas time
Singing, "Silent Night Holy Night"
And a little "Joy to the World"
Merry Christmas 2008
To all men, women, boys, and girls
Now Dear Lord
To you I pray
Please protect everyone
This Christmas Holiday
Remember Jesus is the reason for the season
And the world is lit by his light
Merry Christmas from Joe and Margie
And to all good night

Christmas 2010

Twas the Sunday before Christmas 2010
When all through New Bethel's Church House
Everybody was praising the Lord
No one was quiet as a mouse
The ushers kept their watch
And they greeted everyone with care
Because they all knew that Jesus
Was going to be there
The male choir sang every song
Down to the tee
The musicians were the bomb
Everything was played in the right key
Pastor Fisher was up in the air
And Pastor Branson was too
He delivered the word of God
For both me and you
He talked about issues
And the days to come
Aren't ya'll glad
that Jesus was born
Yes this happened at New Bethel
The Sunday before Christmas 2010
And if God say so next year, New Bethel
We can do it all again

The Sunday Before Christmas 2018

Twas the Sunday before Christmas
When all through New Bethel church house
Everybody was having a good time
No one was quiet as a mouse.
New Bethel's Praisers for Christ
Did their dance to the tee.
While the youth choir and musicians
Played and sang on key.
The Ushers stood their posts
As all the worshipers could be heard
While they waited on The Lord
To send them down a word.
No one could be seen
outside on the grounds.
But praises was going on in the church
And was heard for miles around.
Reverend Fisher would preach
All about the Lord
Because New Bethel Church
Were all on one accord.
Yes, all of this happened
On December 23, 2018
And if you were at church that day
You will know what I mean.

I'm about to end my poem
May your holidays have joy and cheer
Merry Christmas to all of you
And have a Happy New Year.

Margie Hubbard

www.ingramcontent.com/pod-product-compliance
Lightning Source LLC
Chambersburg PA
CBHW062053280426
43661CB00088B/832